THE VOICE THROWER

The Voice Thrower

Tim Allen

Shearsman Books

First published in the United Kingdom in 2012 by
Shearsman Books
50 Westons Hill Drive
Emersons Green
Bristol BS16 7DF

Shearsman Books Ltd Registered Office
30–31 St. James Place, Mangotsfield, Bristol BS16 9JB
(this address not for correspondence)

http://www.shearsman.com/

ISBN 978-1-84861-205-1

Acknowledgements
Thanks to the editors of *10th Muse* and *Shadowtrain* who published
sections of *The Voice Thrower* and to Ben Watson who featured a recording
of part of an early version on *Late Lunch With Out To Lunch*
on Resonance FM.

The Voice Thrower

A poem in 333 quatrains originally written in the
mid '90s then extended and rewritten 2006—
2008 and Autumn 2009

For my mother,
Nan Allen (née Hannah Lawton)
b.1919 Cobh, County Cork, Eire
d.1990 Portland, Dorset UK

Ruby asteroids throb in the back of the throat Wrist
opens knee opens can of tomato seeds spitting split
stitched climactic warning up steady winded steeds
towards a stable environment where copper hearses gogreen.

Everything's perfect then you hear someone exclaim
what the fuck was that? copper insanely copping it as
a torch song 'bout coping gives outunder copying &
throws voice thrower's voice back calling out *comb my veins.*

Inherit and endure thumped crispdust christens Percy
Thrower in the valeoftears throwing up Patsy Palmer
azif the present is a by-pass passing the buck onto ab
original sightseeing Boomeranged poet What will nature be?

galumphing along the lands of the sea shouting *shoot*
Roddy Redrawn's shoddy horizon it'llbea hoot scatty
crest on a scantily dressed canvas of hoe&hod hoody
gorbled sassy dry by sassenach assassin wept into that black

half of the flag We are here for the show take it away
we've come strung-out straight from a cack retail sur
rogate to weave an adjectival way through aristorat's
eczema to the bar where revamped sunspot descends crowing

asifitwas dawn galumphing across English glands for
less than a grand Go fill half glasses with bifocals' at
omic chequebk fogflume lawflaw while a callgirl call
ed *calligraph conflagration* tucks the throat of a hack choking

for someoneelse's art inwhichGlaswegianwitchspeak
s German I swear blind*man* this Eric&Ernie won'tbe
about culture but will beeabout from flower fifteen 2
flower 4 then bee back again in hazy purview compass buzz.

Sleeping sound in a voice box masquerade keeping m
e mum mention free of rushed hoarse Irish palimpsest
testtext theatre heater myth eater circumstantial carpet
beater Hannah Lawton polished the furniture until you could

see the sunset init even though the orb was wobbling
yet up Portland's weird East Weirs in staunched flud
path of boxed-ear sunrise hunted from the frontroom
's one hundred corners of ashen auburn gorged literati Innit?

He read the residue so knewthenew by its helmet hair
cut *and* who he had been to nowhere with wearing 'is
best birthday suit b4 coming back loaded with kaleido
scopic sizzling plastic stones collided with triangular platters

of meat missing season foottrapped in Hades autumn
Arsenal nil auto enigma Georgie-Artaud-Best sprung
untitled from United red slide on icewhite runway of
German strip towards a Liverpool where love was everything.

He avoided her body but couldn't avoid her laughter
Red spirals cracking down to float and blaze-cluster
Her avoided body was a demobbed practical physics
lesson redeemeddead innocent cunningly offcourse ofcourse.

Gravid spectator emptied sozzled antonym into a box
cart spin thru the spinney where her hair snatched ata
spun sun spurting round a humped crow's pumpedup
shadow She delivered him where whisker roost narrows to the

posture of oceanic rootpie epic evilly clubfooting for
ward into scrawn scribbled dribbled garlic deficiency
Temple filament gaolbait sent St. Mike to hoodwink
wankers into barmy army I'm your own definition of identity.

No crisis just a blank passport into purgatory alone to
meown mazement Fresh steak candyfloss bloomed be
tween us and the beasts Professional godz fanninguzz
wiv phaze broom Shy n silent studsigned suburban river tacits.

Drenched in entrenched French Aunty Ancestor fell4
a fullmouth stuffed w needles 4a fullmonth Needless
to say they jet gaga She brings silence to his face but
he customises it Fen congregation rattle all-in fullback to dug

in fells Wewent down the Palindrome every Saturday
nigh danced back2back woefully imprecarious as *are*
intelligence got tattooed by strobe virus butbeblowed
Take that she said *Take that back and shuv it* crawl touch even.

Meshed alley hen fence facilitator or before Anti Eve
pecked her way thru a fevered afternoon in the glassy
white mud of night Exnight towards the end of prude
apocalypse foo hoo Strewn binary isle plasma sampler Fiction

ary of *Dealth* Sanctum moan vacuumed up Go-get an
annulled rechord The ungrateful health's recycled Cy
clops songcycle rationbook of written-off bacon buys
duty-free ballbearings bag knocking socks off their soft swirl

whirling knockedoff marble bookends drowned inink
powder lusty flashfeather off just to madden me mam
wearing Bob Weir festival underwear Festive asylum
sprint printer pegged 10tents out as the hurricane blew in from

14

a property under sub-tropical Dartmoor hothouse blis
ter She was a redhead and he was a deadhead Bunche
s Lay did this lay did that lay trashed some driftwood
Autonomous clerk crunched to crack half a relic into lunch.

Shivering chivalry by proxy Guinevere arrives awry
saying wry things wrong like *silknazipervespasmpee
ved novel streak nurse* Nocturnal idyll-dick in Dickie
Bird's Emporium quay Went to Faber & Faber I thought they

were estate agents but no 'twas barroom archaeology
dullard skyblew blub Shift lucre Butt interstice bulbs
Useless tallow stick A kind of zen sacrifice sorts itzz
elf a snazzy kindness Crude ghost in prison doing press-ups

for the press Humus face at the window scraped off
a human noman Orphic orphans dealt random to arm
the rebels before oven bulge bursts ideally letting the
kids yawn had-it loaves Shag shampoo eyesdown wedged a

homemaid hermeneutic toolbox crammed mean with
mangle swoop Wafer sprite twigged off desire for fat
trauma dawn hangs bras from radiator and rain draws
greyscale rose Japchaps strutting up n down the training film.

We 'ad to reverse out of the reservation like the quiet
est twin distributing deviant space traditionallowance
cauterised nerve collision's shallow grave pastel Add
adverse quote to cosmos fascist philosopher's advertisement.

He looked dapper in braid in an autumn artmag flick
though leaving conflict back home beats heartbroken
masses missing Mass on the Staten Island ferry It's a
reversed apron saucy willy house hubby coffee morninging

on borrowed time If we'regona vote for reincarnation
who's gona be that worm's grandmother? R.D. Laing
singing *Constant Caving*? Gutgold ark disembarks at
dark park gate from Devonport to Victoria Park where I bark

ed at the flowers as glower floundering amid the mar
ginalia of parklife practising being teacher by teachin
Empson to a kid baptised with Guinness for suggestin
Little Sadie's lovely *Restaurant Joke* indigestion was solvent

honour slagged off of summoned animals They under
study for allofus outthere it's gotsodall to do with you
mate coarsely grunt written but you analysed anal sky
to stand-in for heavy weather language outthere so what's the

fuss if the bookie in The Square flooded the tide died
braking intheretoo Mayo's Cafe sloshhightide barked
in there as well Chesil Garage slop marked evening's
stillwet light A butterfly has 2 wings but 1wayup it makes a

3 3 years later as in relatively recently I remembered
baby mayo bottle from the café who sat behind me in
the blackboard Amazon asking why Indians cut an A
mazon's breasts off in a Blandford fest bookplate His fans in

the class joked off their pinking shock he called hims
elf Yammy so I still think black&white National Geo
graphic plates have yams for breasts I can't help how
meanly memes grant gridelin gridiron to recock a precooked

memory King Lud's last catnap on the throne before
spleen keels him over gives gruesome hotchpotched
mead of narcissism necessary to weedredqueen's pot
latch patch in her garden where wonderful red cabbage grows

from abandoned toilet basin into a topiaried Irish Set
ter munching fistfuls of leaf mould eyeing a dirtpoor
porcelain rabbit burrowing hole into MichelinStar on
a noon moon Dictionary definition: scarlet hare squirts starlet.

Avid Voidoids clog each skin-to-skin smack-up to av
oid nicking old arguments or reoffending latest forest
fire doppelganger performing in unreformed school's
make-believe UK otherwise known as Dunk Kirke in jacuzzi

during happy hour up our orchard of cider house tack
Membrane transparency dampens rampant addictions
to expat *poetry our* But hazard But archaeopteryx but
outpop chill lovechild Matildas Then Mass Then a Wyndham

Lewis windup reminds us politics is a westwind from
the Warsaw ghetto Get away from directions let's get
camping gear out an' slash about in imaginary Welsh
Scotland you can forget a future and wallow in the sleepless

hollow of adolescence Uncomfortable little bays with
their own names Curled up fossil too fond of owning
its thoughts fought for legroom in a tentfull of mums'
boys reading on creeping groundsheet that comic aliens come

into it with more dollars than sense Sorry I'm late my
underpants turned Mobius Hedged bet Merlin engine
grotesqued women-priest-rights in tights into bird of
prey trews in shadowpuppet play Oldnag haggles for reserve

ticket to watch Crazy Horse beingbutchered Estrange
spasm turquoise tangerine rangement The Byrds took
acid I imagine they walky inerted on talking water El
Cid orange lizard ate a cable made literal by critical squint at

a cocktail wig flewing through two caulked windows
Wurlitzer goshawk homed-in on witch-bled escalator
Bear crawled from pub the entire north against its kin
Poppies for Vietnam cd avlaffed all night cd have chewed the

cud all night and still had mooed for more i cd av spa
red me wings &donea1000things I'd never chanted to
Osiris before Marooned in saffron sunspecs with now
t else in the ole world except the ole south Pink comet caught

in trawl net by wrinkled old misnomer Mexico washt
up on Chesil's gleaming chinawhite stones Forewarn
ed I pitted thetruth against thereal n waited Scarlet O
'Hara shooting the Yankee sergeant drooling methodically at

her as us old eggs could spot a red spot a bloody mile
off That's not life in the spot it's acting That's not the
real fire That's not actual desire it's the light disguise
of a lady&guy in love with someone else's history of cinema.

Hairday hell *bareheaded in the foot* rare Asimov yell
belling *I've had jaundice Mr Jarndyce* Onspec bridle
stretch clairvoyantly besotted fell face first from Ann
Radcliffe into cross-examination zone by horror truthdrugged

and thickheaded You don't let a heretic sit on a chair
however drab their heresy The Maid threw light on a
chair can't you see? Cousin sly flux tor tier torn from
hearsay torture song Unbutton that unanabaptist lip if caught

out in court pilled-up in a pile-up on the road to Dam
ascus Damn ask us go on what's an experimental did
act like you muckingout the paintshop for for portray
ing to try the sun going down wearing face of a Falkland vet?

So let's pause Take stock Wait for other traitors to cat
ch up the ketchup sun The bench slats drip as the rain
stops we sit outside The Cove our sleeves suck blood
y mary conversation from *comet comments* and *land shanties.*

Oh Jesus Henry Christ Jehanne d'Arque bein' burned
by a stranger's view of Baudrillard Britblueflame bin
ds 10cent guilt to blind red with deaf&dumb10p opra
glasses so please believe this *Say you down there in the hat* sd

Millie Small *Say was it you stagedumbstruck stuckist*
dancing? said skeletal college girl with Dylan tucked
underarm when no adding machine fruit had heard of
him save David&me in our tiltedback blackcap leather blush.

I blushed all the way up Weymouth front We went to
London to see Joan we wore big brimmed hats and ad
renalin grins An only next time at the Albert Hall was
a seriously unexcited John Cage I've still got the programme.

Randomly tuned radio without anyone listening in on
a licensed sponsored silence ok I'm not so impressed
bored yes in Buddhist retreat framed into being art B
urroughs was a diffident metal fish I wasn't too tossed about

but a birthday present from Bill is a movable feast so
I just want Mesmer's eyed stare into its cold ridge of
coal The great can grate monkey nit barbershop gibb
erish to orderly queue ordeal lateagaindawn cora dung indiff

erents Botox sunset goosecheeks chap on sentry duty
Princess Diana doing anew advert for Vision Express
Be at hostess peace as unpredictable as toast or chops
Politics will suck the meat from your health-club brain Just an

other effickly unelffy topcoat His writing's eccentric
twitching in remission but ad hoc blood brother gang
tread down heaven's sticky treat streaking pagan old
gold unembarrassed chaperone clad eager beavers Blood of

Spain Blood of France and the Arctic Cockroach Our
understanding of these things is vague but my vvoice
is clear as mustard oxen groaning surrogate *ahh Bisto*
in the new bistro Disinterred pipe regains consciousness at a

junction in the wind where meaning gets notoriously
complacent Atmospheric art relay of relaxed ratcatch
ing Jackal oratory w'out fear's gloss or nonfict's Viv
Westwood matt on the stairs as Vivienne Leigh shoots grizzly

Yankee sergeant staring through horizontal holocaust
The burning of Atlanta above Tillycoombe canons on
Verne's top tier stuffed with torn Bloom cannons and
Mary Shelley's fossil collection shelling the house 3doorsup

knighting Dad a burning banister hero sungover night
over the road over and above Holy Child Sec's trip to
Longleat then we ran off without saying thankyou sis
to the nuns returning to their convent looking as lonely as Frank

enstein in the middle of the fire behind Tory Amos'
eyes Van Buffalo buffets brig breeze up Van Helsing
making bubbles last&last Descending sungrist Green
Hump hums with effervescent mystery like Everest in the V

oice Thrower's bastard twin Then buffeting shadows
creep from the table as a animal sulks adjective grief
or heapspreads tremulous Then speak*verb*reverb The
n winding sheet clogs the washer disables the dryer therethere

then shine 4th the madmen of Meek Hip shipwreck is
god'sodd way of saying *we're there now* and spiritual
healer's awful tie is an ism saying pattern isn'talways
repetition At the last instant Lizzie Siddal jilted on esplanade.

Sympathy votes for brass porpoise in rusty ballot box
Rusticated socks clean dirty bath smells with Paradox
Inside-out bog brush scrubs torqued Armada nostrum
A proof over our heads A wise teacher with a vicious red pen.

Rammedhome existentialist exists on a slopeless ram
p slopping a plank without corners spreading walkies
w'out dimensions over a sandwich with no bread The
black&red ensign of Anarchy flies off on a conceptual voyage.

Yesterday St. Vulgar cancaned today's burning martyr
b4 tomorrow coz laststandstanza assassinates bleating
hart royalty's insurrection's articulation to tow two to
wers of correction to the head of department's Red Cross box.

The sea's annual holiday to the seaside alone leaves a
yeti footprint to ventriloquist dictat mould Gorbyman
ia reissues *Happy Jack* drum track Zinc waves rigged
up sonar mortis We sawum off we waved down a cystic Hydra.

Nocturnal void and null fodder paves round old field
gun dressed rank for work in news weeds Human bar
ricade more afraid of Descartes than another civilwar
so woke-up my supernatural prayer to the great exhausted one:

Leave mystic fascists behind in their mystical fascism
Dump fascist mystics in their fascistical mystic dump
Pretend mystical fascism is invisible drive on through
throwing back a jealous swearbox at a blackbox recording *it's*

a perfic day for lame animals in the zoo free juzz like
you&me to crawl back in scowling gingerly as Simon
Cowell drawls *anyone here seen Kelly's scrawling bk*
with them illuminated letterheads drawstring dreams navvies

in navy knickers and knackered goldfish? No nobody
's beenseen to fit or else Elsie influences on her knees
Let the world do that letit dothelot letit geton with be
ing world while we unorganise a suicide squad on inorganic

quad bikes *I* which means *merry is the day* saw Julie
Felix on *The Frost Report* singing *Daddy's taking us
to the zoo tomorrow we can be shifty or modest three
times all day* Julie's so happy cheekbones in the studio lights.

Watching the sun go down in thelandoftherisingsun a
little monster lives in the monstrance post-listening to
A-list morse mute rhinestone slabwag Wuby Rax and
Rob Roy join the Khmer Rouge for afterschool drama practice.

Pre-Raphaelite Bros gatecrash craft-fair with enchant
ingly jealous consecrated fraud squad aboard passing
bleeps-in-the-night witness inflamed by gall& rotting
bladderwrack Norman Wisdom abroad SunKing of Salzburg.

Ruthless revision norm 'll no be 'nother toothless Ru
fus Just a piece of dead meat down road apiece stuck
prone upon a platform soul you mused on a way back
from one of Margaret's funerals The moon climbs from trees

as red as a dying sun Widow Sioux scrapes snowboil
for scraps of her cloven-footed daughter who twisted
her head from cavalry officer who stretched her body
straight quoting the deranged godson who died on Calvary for

her sins when its his grinning fuckface what's sinning
pinning her to polished grind backward spunky sequel
grief coming up disjunct trumps Peeing red in moonlit
gallery Tarot pack retaliates wrong rape epicentre slum mum

who can't floss her gums are bleeding that legendary
squirrel war that tore our country apart opening imag
ination to the possibilities of natural admintoss Tardy
lustresnook broke damsondog biscuit woodturned mushroom

carved from sweatrash shoepolish Alice dropped inon
the horse and hid inside to escape a herd of gymnastic
POW's heard em vault over her ears Yfront supermen
pushed into comic punditry on the long&winding Rd to Billy

Butlin's sepia cheeseboard chessboard where a brown
Maoist set fights off red Mounty set riding sidesaddle
through pines like their Queen Camp shop also sells a
Moonies v HMS Bounty set +atleast4more inc. the Bouncing

Bomb v A-Bomb twin-set The other jigsaws shelved
above that short-arsed long-haired bald git over there
eyeing harbour lights whenwhathewants is the whole
set of sets but shopkeeper's a female silhouette w'out lipstick.

Little Annie popped up on the pony brazenly pungent
simulant stimulant incalescent cheeses mudpie quonk
She got herman she smoked out Veruca Salt thwarted
that wart then casually went to war with hotface poker temper.

Flaming tongues havetogo for appraisal by them they
praise Herr Sprak replaces jealous nasally pat zealous
praze Professional curse initiated a wrong roundhead
up&away our alley ceremonial prophesy marvel heresy in the

herenow sally booked for speeding but hewas only do
ing95 on what he thought was an open road to the end
of the world If human skull is pearoid then horse skull
's exterminating protractor axes through makeup core in cock

erel movie remake of highbrow fog modernised nurse
ry Manson mansion repainted elbowroom bruise blue
Lenny le Lion asleep in the corner leaps up in leopard
skin Magritte drops dumbbells on his feet as actresses out of

Margate migrate from marmalade to Marmite then cat
out-of-the-bag majorettes practise marching all March
in Pygmalion prep for busy season kicking Thigh Sch.
dream antics The Devonport chants *get yr stilts out for the lads*

but Major Barbara battens down the hatches to an un
derground attic screen test ad dabs batcellar Subvers
ives adlibbing from an outhouse where hound&horse
scream *Macbeth* to each other in the stab and slash kitchen of

country n western An axe makes a passing remark W
hy quarrel with history Casting director gets credit on
scroll it'sso important to replicate acrobatic symbiosis
Red Queen Neurosis does her own rewiring Jigjump & Dum

pyhump come alive as characters You ain't got Gerry
de Nerval's nerve to ignore all allegoric cerise bosom
pall Blossom dreary belfry puppetmaster pulls preach
er's strings A stretched sermon for the servants an oral history

gone all gothic n whiskery unlike lobster mistaken for
a piggypink walk through blownby flotsam on the old
morning of the planned rebellion It snowed It knowed
it would The King's carriage stuck in slush instead of sticking

another oar in sentimental carnage It bucked off liver
slipper It biographed with a home-grown metronome
Negative equity auction in glade shade of mock Span
ish convent cancelled by Council A brash new hospice built

itself uphill Flamingo those lungs undo idling salmon
wrung rareringtone Evil medicine cabinet remembers
medicine ball's birthday Desks at dusk knockin blood
orange heads together Caligari cabinet government garrotted

a rotten candy carrot for a Judge Stickler sticking stub
born with whatheknows then picking at whatheknows
til the blood flows So a double-jointed donkey isn't so
double-jointed *so?* Used only by poets and interior decorators.

Winches inch rich into firestorm finchfollow-through
the yard though it's as fluid ounces as absurd acres of
area burnt by litres without a metre and yes I can mix
that one for you Sir you won't get 'em mixed up once they're

mixed Church is dragged out to the circus on the edge
of town where the sun goes down Hoop an arrow in a
row with dead-centre hopes instead of shooting a still
growing arrowhead through a poolhall loophole Aim it blind

at a hatching salmon catcher Hold your spanked hand
in front of your mouth then amplify the redskin holler
by doing what we did as kids did for Foucauldian tree
felling shamanic Irish tics The whole town gets shod to race

on hoofed stilts Shed Irish ancestry by your own effin
effort in the fold-away name of a lifeboat holding hut
Peter O'Toole's winslet is a pastoral tool as The Titan
ic sinks into race memory supporting Everton through a celtic

twilight window wearing Liverpool red at a *Match of*
the Day supper of swiglets & cider Skirl passion gurn
oesophagus sore Sheffie score on the wrong weekday
Laugh at bowls over beast in lacquered anthology lapsover.

An ant wanders downtown with a shamed shaman ash
amed on the rack flapping a harangue A kitsch *naught*
ies 'cordin to whose boss A couple of so-called social
skills weather fronting rightwing personage and a new prime.

Leafing through a railway cutting an old papercutting
tunnels through numinous Weymouth as-easy-as-you
like memory to agonize over exaggerated imperatives
Don't concern yourself the alchemist will call when he's crack

ed it Disinfecting sprinklers edit-out our ceiling Cont
inental drift virtuoso beefbulbous dry reefy faxes nub
ile bile to mobile a stone'sthrow from the capped hor
izon's 4 gotten mobbed forest floor oceans plus a new crime.

A horizon was 12 miles away We counted generously
Any remaining mile clocked circumstantial dozing on
duty like frozen dew blocks of meditation on Bergson
's duration Fanclub minibus fitted-out by deconstruction work

ers in soft hats and invertebrate scaffolding or just for
a mo an animal without a body tailed out of my mind
What I had in head instead was as civilised as an Ash
bery drifting abstractly through parkland in a city of suncloud.

So Y this violence Y logical positivist frisbee fatigue
Y croc caged as ifit was fate and Y does the Yea Yea
Yea's *Y Control* on car tapedeck soundso weedy? We
half know answers but not Y tonight's pub quiziz cancelled.

Circus-free anemone spots Einstein on a melancholic
refresher course curving off melon into star struck in
sulation Insidious audience cheek is now a nation puf
fing orders to stockbroker braced for the turning of the Earth.

Closing market cafe's mark-ups brought bought tears
Red Square stamp trade radicalised by traditionalised
found object aesthetic branded lux sense recompense
Dilated facial muscle discovered at *There Might Be Martians*

Funfair where one pollinated Mary sideshow is an in
tercession by the virgin lily pad on behalf of any pun
ter at least trying to levitate a crate Mary says *I could
n't breathe swimming with a plesiosaurus for pure pleasure.*

Payday's never same day shy at work will say *no one
texts Rex for puréed pleasure* Pray*ery* portmanteau/x
fingerdip art auction erupts in an inexperienced salad
dripping Villa beetroot A veranda moment with butch slaves.

Artisans' quarters scribbled on yet another surface of
a universe of colour samples e.g. *BadlandGullyGulch
Cherry Chrome* gum powder dried in rusty tin David
and me buried with mum's jewellery in a time soaked quarry.

Negated variety verbatim pearls cultural glut but it do
n't stop glutenfree phraseology from dabbling jobs on
the side drum Concert psychoanalyst don't know what
to make with the elements no bugger's jacket tail .com.org.or

event horizon to high-tail to to wit swig a swordswall
owed swagdraw to switchfool Archie *Andraws* on the
radio knocking back carrot juice as shrill prelapsarian
laughter is canned for the first A vampire backbites Rudolph

but Rudolph bites back the bat changing back into an
old man answering the door I took that from a SATS
practice paper After-fear of powerful fools' tools hav
ing long since festered into a personalised witchcraft smelling

of me mind Milk floats from a syntactical party game
flummoxed by diddly squat project The subject came
up like vomit from flexiglass tumtickled by agile frag
mented personality couched as Darwinian crisis management.

Pork then morepork across the swirling waters where
the Amorphous forks they can moor then afford to dr
ift downstream trying to understand how in *Dallas* M
iss Ellie could change so completely Her voice tinted orange.

Affordable or not the Utopian Bank gives us a rave re
view The staff wave In roads Rerave Acedown on yer
sleeping partner's face Went to see *The King and I* 3 t
imes with cousin Kevin inheriting pocket money motitivation.

Went with Kevin too to see *Modern Times* long times
ago The Single Story Cinema next *The Holy Ground*
once more quipped on a chill quality of evening light
queuing equipped with Cork Harbour boathook Charlie Chap

lin lived in an empty telegraph station on Atlantis On
cue coach approached a white haired philanderer who
couldn't speak *stillwaterdeepkeepsake prescient sand
dune* Expression late as usual Algebra learns it's not Scrabble.

Lost playfully lost at the pantomime of sad oddities F
rom coach window fret is that a brick brewery or old
railway station? The questions of childhood retrospect
ively rhetorical Verbs in credit must cag*ed* wait in their heavy

weight ice hockey gear for any old new noun's unem
ployed chic Abandoned balance bandage book enters
novice's knocking shopped novel as coy libertine bric
-a-brac and excessive crabbed ribald grovel escalated to a moot

point dressed as a rather needy Adam & Eve Eden ad
vert stretched towards a full stop then stretchered off
the page So to did history gradually degrade into a ra
ther daft field event Jester's gestural pitch inside the O2's tent

black fireworks Doomnaked I admired the man perch
ed on Eros waving banner saying *Blair is a cunt* I see
the solar wind sweeping through his scruff he looked
indeed in need of a meal and wash but what the hell I agreed.

Sculpt 0.9 pintsize pinchednosed adventure in *Who's*
Who sotto voce sottisier directory went in direction of
besotted insider history in Minister's redbox scuff full
of laundered sotadic catalogues *in manner of catalectic tetra*

meter of ionics Answers hardlined a Nirish Euro brag
ging poetaster as he scoured the diablo coast befriend
ed by tabloid creationist in stuck lift unable tobreathe
sums *UUthere inthehat yesU comehere andbe MyBoyLollypop.*

Only when the lift broke down did we break down as
well When a hole opened all imaginings were sucked
down Only then did we notice the lift-shaft was lined
with wallpaper Hell is just a wall away from hanging root con

stipations Set out to teach the class Venndiagrams put
dress designer in 1 hoop he's no sociologist put socio
path in hula-hoop intersecting man in a cafe scooping
his lifestory to a select group in a restaurant while the class re

class classwarp chalk tally I pushed I tried to shuvum
out of their class while giving them pride in what they
were being pushed from I'll never know if any of this
worked leaving behind me a cold soup memory of love&hate.

Eat bloody burger in the street straight from the brief
case Scratch Gauguin classes from soiled briefs an A
rt Brut archaeological alfresco freak-out forelock tug
Gather round Gallagher brothers aiding Roland pick his pony.

Penguin Classic of Eric the Red found Klondike gold
in Tottenham bedsit1972 lunched in Greenland Co-op
with Bren&friend Rosie's pale palaeontologist hubby
hominid specialist always on telly with a Yorick in his hands.

Open to folio a talking birthday card sings barbershop
reading scheme for trio of 4leafed clovers roosting on
spire of spruced-up Xmas spruce overseeing privateer
polio buck heaven hierarch lipstream stymie Angel dandruff

coats covenglove playing gooseberry rasp on *Seatops*
Insert alluvial dandruff Insert jazz exam Insert a slick
of consciousness into the deadtext Insert an advert fo
r irksome earthend privigrief ritual pulling bullock by his ball

oons it's Heaney and his Da inebriate Swinburnesque
celebs Tie a yellow ribbon round the old hokum of no.
2billion&3 Memory Lane usedtobeknown in Navy as
houseyhousey I name this houseboat Honōrificābilitūdinitātibus.

Breathe in through the window butout through a door
Relieveweathywidow'swreath not believing anymore
Rude red windy Dao blows out Totnes Castle candles
Turn style propaganda monsta hauling lobsta basket basking

in rosé twilight Not sure if this shore is the right shore
Felt left scalding seaweed hoary white Green eyeliner
humps the Green Hump's boiled thighs ofsea engross
ing me Landslipped quarry boulder debris shyly slips a cool

hand in a hot hand-held pulls 2 parallel futures down
1 quaked nightdrill secretly gaping gospel flitkiss fan
cydress ball bouncing along West Weirs to the Hope
ofBadLuck where clay lies exposed & silhouettes must marry.

Heading southalong West Weirs with our hair on fire
Knotted look-no-hands stuffed up puppet's arse tonsil
echo She sits on his lap smiling at a sea's indifference
though no plough could tug through gorse hair for a *yezpleaze*.

Dylan spotted his bundle of joy *down along the Cove*
Mystery creation missed rosarybead uncovered an ad
ult audit in the *yes me lud* child a cliché maybe but so
true as in *sooo truuue* I don't have the Dr's sonic screwdriver

but I do have a pair of secateurs and enough blood in
my mouth for boaf ovus Comic ditto's in the detail in
aversion Juliet fell on retractable sword while Romeo
scrabbled in a dictionary until he fingered the weightlessness

of an evening in the Ardennes Nothing nihilistic jump
s you yet as the rest have already eaten you buy a bun
dle of software in military hardware shares whenallwe
really want is to share Bunter's food parcels of cherry-picked

raspberries Don derrière chopper flamethrowerrocker
Dracula in buckskins even more erectile down acidic
aisle He was no acid-head though no but a sessile ten
tative head-rhyme The air in here's frou-frou and as jaundiced

as a top-heavy sky round the ankles A rustic romance
screaming through a love tunnel gawping at the walls
The East Weirs were where we was when an easterly
were so cold you had to hold your ears It cut a path through a

packet of Navy Cut penetrating restricted access pass
The barbed wire hadn't changed its t-shirt since 1940
Hovercraft bounced past a graceless arthritic hare and
dogged morning sickness by not sending its dolphin to school.

There were always further worlds over the horizon be
yond Hardy's Monument but places were quaint word
pictures of hoardings bordering a clean-cut thrown-up
through road cake Made-to-measure factory made maids make

measurements of mathematic instruments And across
the street the dairy where I worked Sundays washing
out milkbottles on a washing out milkbottles machine
I smelt sour I was saffron pages in my copy of *The Waste Land*.

OK sky at first-light as yellow as a teddybear belong
ing to T.S. Eliot's favourite Lear christened Thyroid
1st propped on spanky new kitchen units just like thy
self supine on golden worktop taking workshop on anaesthesia.

Teddybear Teddybear climbs a tiara called *Gobble D.*
Gook Teddybear Teddybear pants yobbish prayers as
the sun goes down or praps they're prayers to yobs to
go yob elsewhere Selfish ideology bluntly breeds a billionaire.

There's too many rhymes up there their airiness gives
the false impression of correspondence but there ain't
no unembarrassed way to talk about the richman's im
morality solet'slet Apple*aps* chord miserymort Demolition site

dragonfly saw postie comingintolandon marshmallow
flyforward citing crusade creep anglocatholic masque
as plain as a plain from a plane Map no bordered fold
gruel crease rough contour A Wednesday tour bus wends with

evacuee blitzkids to Bilbao Tossed bedbug caber toss
ing careerist never took his wife to a howff houf or h
ouff but his woof tagged along like a little joke token
in the largely enjoyable world where the Great War can carry

on as a pub club Shepherd's delight pie charts Ann R
obinson hoodooed grub ghettoblaster nuver parochial
parkingmetre hooded&bound by convolvulus stained
glass asschapel intheghetto catching last light of Pelvic King.

Musical palsybard at eisteddfod bar impersonates fey
taff elves parley pound rump 4pound if not prompted
Russ Conway took his piano to his dentist and said
take them all out I've seen the light it's called John Cage as silent

as moonlight through a bird cage but artists are cruel
daubers Peter Piano said *ughgirls ugh* I still didn't ca
tch on he'd never heard of The Stone Roses when we
watched a herd of My Little Ponies thunder from Dartmoor sky

line shaking our buns He loved Erasure though it still
didn't click maybe he loved me too How's that make
me feel? Yorkshire perhaps I feel like Yorkshire with
out its cities & dales like Atlantis with a dry cough in August.

Royal fever exiled half-dozen rabid haiku from a pack
of red clubs&spades Mr Blobby quarantined in casino
loses what's blabbed loose in blotto Bashō translation
but the lonely individual human is subjected to hair-splitting

dissection like Bashō's frog in skip dye Biology bash
ed-in in art room science hop Colours bled thrift van
dal thrust through metaphrased practice throw Chuck
observed object up Freedom Rd. to skimpy jumpster powwow.

Stay poz The roads of freedom are the roads toorfrom
freedom they goddabe Have you seen my saw no but
I seen a man take a sledgehammer to a waste bin then
I saw him drop it in giving ingredients a good stir for a goldstar

from *Daemon Headmaster* Writing nolonger tiptap re
vision the tongue constructs a lighthouse on landfill s
eparating tall stories with ventilation plagiarism inthe
desert necropolis built for the expected plague of Jesus freaks.

Puppeteer scours the bins out back of the doll hospital
which shares a dress with a hedgehog hospice address
donated by Militant to Milbank *Your aving a retro lau*
gh Recycled Heraclitean hogroast confesses she cross-dresses

hisself cross the road knowing no whizkidcar pazzing
fazt is ever the same 1 When you've seen 1 unknown
gnome put down as roadkill you've only seen a single
stat The roundabout featured the ark animals plus a few others.

Copper hiding in Eden's undergrowth milk-stains uni
form with *Pictures of Lily* Not an original sin in itself
but chewed gubblebum inkwell vortex valentine lyric
straying onto a national contract with overqualified police dog

getting rid into sunset by concentration camp guard A
man as was once came out of the camp singing or gig
gling not sure which he didn't know he was singing&
giggling he thought he was explaining stuff by asking innocent

questions of tiny mites who'd never set eyes on a hor
izon *is Nazism the optimum of chaos order?* but none
reply they're conscious corpses they weedkill nought
about nuffin as far as they know the world could be a graphic

novel made of placemats laid by tiny creature-crumbs
coasting organised illustrated chapter stair touched up
in Lincoln Cathedral where slotted into breathlessfear
between shop-soiled missals I found poetry pamphlets by souls

I edited underumbrella of *Unmolested Mole Dentures*
Space Cult haven't room to park the spaceship before
their monthly meet in the mouth of a family planning
clinic where stoned single mums marry foul multi-storey flat

bed copiers convening to rent anarsoned beach chalet
Instructions emblazoned on fire extinguisher *Inmates*
in partyhat lonely nimbydrill I pinched Anne Frank's
diary from her satchel and read it playtime I went as red as a

red horseshoe on an autumn evening Unhinged music
ian falls through door he's painting using orange peel
Export biz falls for carrot-top field in deserted garage
forecourt Garrotted pump leaks ipso-facto filtersplead storm

petrolbled nuptial Throwing a sicky drivinginstructor
throws in introductory lesson to Barthes' *Camera Luc*
inda It's true I'm literary yet a little illiterate in fact I
'm neither since throwing my voice off in a library's *shuushh.*

Rhythm through bored librarians into mime Resort to
undercover disco Rediscover lowbrow culturecrewed
*Godot*thrash raven-on-the-backleg rawdeal grafted to
plastic chair in plastic surgery waiting room with embarrassed

booty No mean queen on this team not even my mum
atherangriest no this is consultingroom insult blushed
lush Elizabethan crimson goblin globulin Drake Prim
ary Sch. horsemeat in refrigerated lorry heads arse-about-face

to Highbury cattlemarket unloading sentimental drain
pipe psychoanalysis of dramaqueen the Bonzos know
what I mean gets thrown through boobtube to emerge
in a forest clearing where the greenman rehearses pantomime.

Flushed out Hermit frog makes association after Asc.
e.g. his nephew sitting on the stairs watching a lady's
dress make an off-the-rail film of what's up tramlines
to para-zenith is tramping into town to get a seedy Cramps cd.

On thebusback a dog lay dying in bloody road his tail
wagging but no one at an end of long traveller's string
trailing him Wrote about this play elsewhere on stage
of earlier this The bus carried on up North Hill as if driven by

Solzhenitsyn Depressed by cliché and confident cool
of those less talented I maybe butav never had one of
those poem bonfires in the back yard or shredded any
evidence yet carry on as if I was a doggie branded with the ©.

Baby thrownout with dismal baptismal douses smoke
signal from vanity case in barrelblaze but dive deeper
into thumped tub commissioned art-work for familiar
echoresonancerelevancesubmission&decommissionedmeaning.

The lights is on amber the insects are trapped for ever
Excavate a zero with little more than a kid's inhuman
noise and a piece of string from Lenin's speech at Fin
land Station The Little Moor takes a little more from eternity

if there's room but there never is 'cause the Universe
wears a dead soldier's uniform &thingslikethis reflex
thatasifitwasfact the actual act of a slackskinned basil
isk's radial starch Our eyes&ears steadfast in the face of The

Prodigy who are kwite filosofical but hardly sublime
plume ranter Burne-Jones toss Undercurrent kiln rent
loss litigates quince riot dance sequence retina spume
stock Filing cabinet tied to kite found undisturbed at rainbow's

end If I've got a criticism of Derrida it's that he's 1 of
a 100 people who don't know who Joe Brand is but I
haven't Pastry struggled 3 from chickpea pasty couch
potato Cromwell come armchair intellectual *Eastender* Keith

vegetated but if I've got a criticism of any soap opera
it's that I can't find one neither is its dirty dish dished
slopmelted beetroot but when Keith's parsley fell free
from pastry facecream stuck sponge in jam n ststastammered

'caus the jam was ham Lear The Munificent Lear The
Inkblot Sphinx Lear Impassable Coherence Lear Of S
low Light Lear Psychic Walker Lear The White Glass
Anybody a chancer held down like a criminal under the entire

cast of *The Bill* We struggle free incidentally but slats
of ply pursue you through rural deprivation priviwood
blocked gill tickle ohwell chase&embrace I'dsrrender
if decaying in the dark unable to breathe passed rats I'm peep

ing through at the peak of romantic terror that's a cab
lecar sunset G*luv*puppets dangle profane optic prayer
mats Nightmare threwyouawake into the exaggerated
3rd planet then veryvery vertical on the horribly horizontal you

learnt their luvheart lingo Deep ecology slithers from
chimney2chimney with last year's presents swapping
one Gaia joke for another then cracks rocks as a wind
decorates itself with molten medals awarded by a particularly

garrulous Confucius next Mayday We're devorstated
lebensraum omen openwound We used to walk every
where some places we even ran to too singing mostly
everything in our native tongue doing *good god* impressions.

Simpering cataclysm outsourced catechism scavenge
or similar with Wittgenstein wit we could convert the
human obstaclerace to odds-on favourite but naughty
aught to have taught us thisatleast there ain't a glorious sunset

without an imagination getting burned Sunflowers pre
tend being lasagne artists Antibiotics play boxing mat
ch weigh-ins Isolation ward radio bombshells a bloom
into spring Boom lean across to lick my brow makes my heart

a-flutter Demon whinged on about his home life as if
I cared I nodded halcyons back at him e.g. where I'm
from hedges are the wage-earners the harbours are cr
ammed full of jamtarts and cats queue-up business-like for 1st

communion Wily on subject eating out in Limbo ed
ited-out maul lectern notch panned surveillance while
we nap Who focuses there state your business brawn?
Maypole snaps in the late afternoon light of a cold May morn.

Snap decision during cold snap warmed by Schnapps
Grail dandy beknights writer's plot-grid knocking ba
ck lunch on weeknights The lockup smellsofSarson's
Mercury's flaccid mismatch goes to hobby credit scab+ maudlin

audit pause 'cause My mother's selfless anagram catal
ogues her analogues I haven't seen her since1990 and
that wasn't really her or her homonym or hyponym In
the wanton underworld the damprat wants for nothing Nothing

gets done down here Edgar Allan P and Baudelaire ex
change a bored glance and the occasional wet fart reo
rchestrating jazz into columns of cohyponyms Beasts
they tell us have no self-image or the means of self-harm a bit

unlike the *thought-fox* chewing off more than it wants
to survive criticism Ted wouldn't put up his brolly he
wishboned to feel raw and wordless An umbrella is a
put-up job Fabian hothead's impatient nature not ideology nip

ped across to Countess Dracula's with plasma packet
The NHS is safe in her glands shapeshifting between
trusty adverse camber towards the galactic centrefold
so don't go giving too much meaning to the meaning of words.

Swathed In Thesaurus enters pawnshop with Wilbury
s' album a frog shaped coughsweet and demolition or
der *The dreams swathed* him there is no better phrase
With heart in your mouth take liberties with cosmo code gobo.

Remember red carbolic not all memory is nostalgic I
lifebuoyed years later while escaping Dystopian stew
by pretending to be a burnout local in phonebox soap
box learnt in phonebook poobin red Linguistic striptease or ars

on? Heathen gorse or weather ablaze motorcycle skid
across moors ending up upended stage scenery on the
first&lastnight of an awful stone row musical that has
no music to speak of to cushion rap in the operating surgeon's

ears as he bounces his interns off the walls on *Casual*
ty The TV is malaria but TV is a quadratrix list Don't
adjust your *Set* as if the father of phenomenology was
a hurly-burly hurling player and not Husserl as a young sea trout.

Metonym the Greek philosopher got a curtain call thr
ough a colander Fen Shi in reverse in Tony Harrison'
s dad's house Ventriloquist bubble expatriates St. Pat
from reptilehouse Prospector gulps expectorant then pops dow

n Cliff Richard looking for Clifton Gorge Once Gary
&me went window cleaning with rungless ladder and
shityellowshami Cling to the summer repeats on rock
face Gently twist flag over the Vatican gents through a wring

er it comes out redder than the Red Army mother raw
knuckle ride Buñuel tapestry occludes sunset thread
by thread Bourgeois Pink Floyd fool slapped-up crap
concert wall Warning threat taps smoulder on shoulder Half a

Guinness&chips sits between Cox and Syd Barrett on
the bench The sun goes down again Strephon expects
a surprise Pippinpip dropped into mazeshade between
pebbles Apricot babe in an autumnal April stomahaze colophon.

Every day is the *Day of the Triffids* for the lighthouse
keeper How many light bulbs does it take to change a
surrealist? My mum wanted me to speak properly she
didn't want me sounding like the other island urchins she failed.

Gullfruit boatrat and girlflesh in a rhizoid ray of light
Boatfruit ratflesh & girdlegoo on a rhizoid raft of lite
Has anyone here seen helium or hydrogen forthat mat
ter Tarbaby basket fledge Shaftwater's sinew flèche patterslog.

Frayed lynchlawyer 'fraid of sly deads' quasichart fla
yed granite gringo vein greengrass banjo James Gang
charted backwaterbullies to hog a corner of the comm
unity hall *We cun make you dance Untie yr laces w bullets for*

fingers &watchyousing No I don't mean here nobody
can hear a thing the gallows humour asthick as police
canteen camaraderie covers the tanner with glory Ran
k deucegrid soliloquy races ivy Zendog stares left through holy

cow The only independent bookshop left in town was
run by somewhat depleted stock version of Salmon R
ushdie but twasstillhim he'd loads of booksabout fish
ing&Egyptology Another crank Rushdie clone ran the cramped

little Devonport library like the bloke in *Black Books*
sneering clear when I let lose kids from Marlborough
Primary into read the pictures Christmas red from the
bitter wind that blew down the concrete channels and enflamed

with temper after I'd guided the crocodile around the
urban swamp There were never people about nobody
had cars the empty streets echoed with the screaming
competition between me and them I've never written about this

why now? His snooty disapproval of my refusal to qu
ell their unruly hunger turned me inside-out I imagine
his relief showed phew when we'd gone back through
the alleys to playtime hell and cold coffee This was slow death

of all inward into outward leaving just a thin layer of
insulation between ideological daydreams of the past
and the dread weave of the present Failure revived an
urge to survive w'out salary thru the post of structural futures.

Revolutionary fantasy surprises itself by becoming a
keen G.I. It's those b&w wars still filmingin the head
grub waking on rind rubbin feelers then 'mediately re
hibernating snugtruck squaddycamp Jekyllsnuffle lampsnaffle.

Tongue-for-a-scarf voice-over invites the neighbours
in4 bellyboulder tumbledown rhetorical gristle The A
4 evangelicals unfold whatever juxtaposed position's
been chucked 'em Listen for the poisonpen beep of swallowed

sub foolscap cylinder bean frottaged isobathic so so o
cean structured likeyou&me and the golden calf glow
ing weirdly infrared The book search for Lenkiewicz'
s copy of *The Famous Five* becomes a book prowl on HMS Sea.

Poisson walk w'out geometry in phosphorescent nud
ity Quantum shadow of Saint Sloth hung like raining
worryballs silhouette ghostdancing up Braillechannel
sewage system worming its sluggish heave to away day at Flam

bards Harvest moon nightwatch caught out on a lim*b*
inal then dropped from team coach outside Brit Muse
um's ethical trove whist drive He [random vagabond]
ignited her [Liz 1ˢᵗ] liquid nitrogen hair from an allotment shed

surrounded by bed of rocket lettuce Bemelted curfew
quarry caught last sherry marble mural of the behead
ed sun Quarantined sharkmeat leper at fire-eating fin
als longfore impostor put Lacan's 1ˢᵗ words in *Tommy's* deaf

ear 2 new romantics at bus stop like prostitutes under
a lamppost don't know what they were waiting for it'
sover 20 years ago 1 could've been cavalier or clown
&his mate a tomtomboy pirate shaved to highlight the time of

day Avoiding 101yr. apprenticeship in 101 Nightclub
I redream my understudy's performance vividly verse
d under-rehearsed reversed hearse ƎƆИA⅃UꓭMA let
ter slide across rear mirror spitfire piloted by vampire juvenilia.

Slandered prankster transfers blister cluster to tabloid
youngsters loving the half-dark's harsh *Illuminations*
Rimbaud's one of them a pale sloven up for anything
including French A level & angelically ruddy cheeked Eng.Lit.

Catherine Wheel councils traumatised bluebell under
cavefloor trying on Plato's Masonic regalia over skin
tight science Cash-creation compensation hereinafter
dermdoc The2heads listening betterthan1 heard war declared

on the school secretary's radio but us teachers picked
itoff the grapevine the pupils already knew their dads
'adsailed off into a sunset on HMS Aircraft a city with
its own shopping chapel Yo*mping Jack Flash* tore into a Dart

moor tor with abseiling bayonet and in the bay below
done to a crisp Welshmen were brought from the bur
ning boat while the camera looked other way towards
the last blackface miners Shushedup inflatable troublemaker

sluices ravaged averages from washed-out Jungian un
able to cut into his habitual parking space in his son's
ZorrosuitsoZorro slashes across Zoroastrianism it'sjus
tabunch a hooligan ideas spitting romance language in the pub

lic toilet councilhouse pinkmintgreen A July 17th sun
plucked a rainbow we played&played&played as if a
birthmark could fringe racket a pocket of keepsake re
treats Hysterically French uppercase Italian baptised by a pop

up Polish spiv pope blessed a dish of nettles &a bowl
of corks for anungry Hibernian willing to lick the lot
clean if&when he wakes from his drunken sex sweet
smear of a dream in which using Smarties for make-up morphs

into beachcombing publicbaths with a Freudian metal
detector that interprets anything it confects as a glorio
us solar bleed Random 9th heat wave transfers Cathar
junk to cloud9 clandestine chapelbabble if it don't makemuch

difference reckoning how to tack havoc's failsafe take
um bystorm sunspotty neonipper to riproar spirit gone
tactlessly cipher cold The carnival comes to town tow
ed by toads the size of rhinos straight from *Melmoth* into Wey

mouth with Van Vliet's *Bat Chain Puller* dragging an
cient Egypt through Melcombe Regis on tiptoe bristle
dopedarts St.Sebastian style armageddoning on empty
wrestling trashbags turned to rusting corrugated Meltis Fruits

applied as rouged CV for the interviewee sieving past
butchery through a false-lashed memory What isn't a
vista buried 'neath floorboards jumpstarts a sequence
of cheesecake and testosterone The accent escaping from the

comedian is a prisoner on shore-leave Voice Thrower
makes concerted effort to glottal stop Inexorable light
jails jealous love in its ribcages then redistributes scab
ideology mongst distant relatives' hare teeth and eyelip Krish

na or whatever on this 13th Friday of Never Crusader
comes home late to the Cannes film fest Crusader co
mes home late from the Cannes film fest I like either
longas utopian orphan gang organise a Ubuqueen debtworld

where Queen Pea isn't a cruelly used paperweight but
tuttut 1 mustn't let regret fester get out there censor &
metagrobolize those pearl1 certs Fictive culture name
frames frozen equation for us misconceived smidgens of pea

santry up the Pear Tree by lunch dressed as pheasants
More should/could be said about this&that if this was
n't under vers libre restrictions but you'd need to stop
really stop what you're seeing as the roller coaster halts hangs

beneath its rail I was always scaredycat when it came
to anything to do with gravity the longer the queue at
Alton Towers the better Once at apex of a waiting for
punters big wheel a sweaty westerly swung our sick swingseat.

Parental perfunct quill kinky hirsute doddlerunt down
grade feature Anchorman intuitively hands over to his
adjunct with rearguard splash Brassband rednecks ren
der their rousing Yorkshirepud version of *Red Sails in the Sun*

set to a right shower of White Guards while the marq
uee pavilion burns to Billy Idol's *White Wedding* sun
g to the tune of *Does Your Wig Loose its Authority on
the Bedpost Overnight?* Glam hierarchy fetishes urban squalor

playing lame rooster blues reveille Infants of all persu
asions sproutpoutspout foursquare on four-poster post
ed on the web by a postman who'sonlygot four posters
on his walls 1 an advert for his friend Vince's version of *The*

Da Vinci Code smuggled out of Vichy France in a hur
dygurdy the other3 areallof M. Magdalene sucking an
iseed balls dancing with Parma Violets at the *Masque*
of the Red Death (the film not the story the sweet not the ham).

Franz Marc's purple herds trample fauves at rave exit
to duck alone on new moon with a beak bright brown
Plastic hoof throbbed like a swollen young balloon in
an unopened pack of taste-buds at Plathblood Daisy Gut's an

aemic party press squashed into insipid insanity but *R*
un paint run run said Beefheart's *Barnaby Rudge* riot
ing gaily deep up NaturalSystems Street with topknot
snatch picking at his stopwatch going to work mildly excited

by dressing up in burst bladders listening to The Dam
ned painting *New Rose* in the under stairs cupboard in
76 The paint dried for 3 minutes while my heart raced
back&forth between decades but the brain stayed-put trying to

invent a neologism it leaked into the earth through no
fault line of its own ragamuffin tug-of-war still going
on after the reeve's rope broke Breakdown break-up+
cancer of the bowel I've had Pandora's jellybaby share Peter

Middleton's dad stepped outside his door into sunbath
then went back in to die not the poet for heaven'ssake
who I saw read I've heard lots of children read plots&
never lost the prose I've heard adults read poetry too wonder

ing what it would smell like if I listened closer I heard
myself read once I didn't like it 'cause it wasn't really
me Dogs don't hear any horizon slide into a city scree
Dogs smell their master's voice no matter how far it's thrown.

Maddogs&Englishmen scribble eccentric opinions in
the visitors' book like *grafix giggle suckup hologram*
butI've never done anything like that it would be daft
Minister of Ubiquities lay shy aside blackeyed Blondel strum

ming his springs waiting to join some blandindieband
but4now he gags on his visitor's kiss licks their shoes
and strangles himself with his own haemorrhoids Off
contiguous huffy afluff off nuffing to eat cept liquorice and a

little nurse to sit on him Munificent ooze offof a Miss
Ellie even orangerthanearlier with contrast too angrily
high off on another one Put gogs on to read flame thro
wer instructions its patent trapped in the pillbox by Alf Garnett

reciting Patience Strong Michael Harvey threw shard
of glass hard from pillbox dirtdark to slit my knee op
en to its anatomical shock vomiting atoms from Eden
seedscatter endgame soulskitter Frankenstein blackberry ripe

right up his arm asfarashecouldreach operating on the
innocent in the undergrowth Lambkin stitches itself a
guiltskin goat coat betwixt bluecoat and redcoat bunk
gunk at the crucifixion of an anteater across the dashboard of

a christian country gone hinduvoid voodoo Ironic that
something so abstract should shiver revealing snowof
fs in shun sign The day they crowned Gregarian pope
it showedup on calendar as a reminder to go for the blood test.

Enschedule means worthless of low birth The last seg
ment of sun segues into stale survival of oilspill Hallo
ween apple-bobbing up with bruises as black as burns
bubbling below the surface of what remains of modern history

though the set texts in the bookcupboard unbind cartil
age bitbybit Education's the slippy side of a Class ZC
submarine it can't pick anyone up it has no hands it's
Penlee Sec. in a sub-pen turned into the lifeboat it's named aft

er but far too late for the Bram Stokers boiled alive in
its bowels Now we're in metaphor's digestive system
call it Edc. policy stuffed with torpedo wadding or zu
nk seaman torpor stroke incubus waiting for the last bus omit

ting quarks ferried from soul by bi-cathartic syntax go
ne to pot the flowers in sulphur Generation X irritates
the hell out of veteran talking to himself *when will the*
ruddy sun go down? When it's reddy says his drowned mate

they laugh&laugh a final look at entrails in an Xrated
trailer they take orally warily traddy in slaughterorder
b&w c&w cowpoke tartanlouse wee thinktank mouse
kept in a tertiary college's labrat metaplasia 'til the kids come

sugarlumping back on Monday More freckles pickled
upon the maniac than highhairlights of the greengreen
lass of home Suspended starpupil falls into lighthouse
lens takes redfaced responsibility for sacrificed shipping lane.

Planetarium chillroom fathomdim limbo cradle rocks
past programmed doggerel bramble grown grubby ac
ros concrete campsite Neap Shoppe Hopidoll synthes
izer reproducing Vera Lyn on violin I recognise the organist's

generic ginger beardbiscuit bending with *Trend* wind
carrying psychedelia off clumsyMod seafrontsprayed
into dancehalldeathwall his broadback a mindwarped
cloakroom ruckus tickbox fat Red Riding Hood's 1st time of the

month has her furrier wet&warm beneath the poultice
moon stillborn under wraps of contagious Fourierism
The Slits fostered-out to houses on fire at the smarmy
end of an anointed hour waking fannyfree from slumberbum

numbnumber gules guise mummer rather too familiar
falsidical quodlibet An alphabet wout AnnieApple or
her apron full of Cox Fan-based gurucrat fashions fas
cist false bottom in bureau still farting Ezra Pound's gas bills.

Ari Up Atlantic reflects wout recollection a socialism
for 4 fishermen of any colour shaving off their beards
with a razored kite string singing *Father oFather why
hast thou not foreskinned me or pinned a woodwork medal up*

on me when talentlesstitch Tim Allen got both just be
cause he persevered with that book rack for his mum
&dad Come true dream reflux sanding a Rosicrucian
horror garagegarden cumofage Compensate rusty cow with a

fag at both ends a black&tan learning Russian from a
calfskin pocket dictionary that squeezes International
Brigade prisoners onto register present butnot correct
then shoots them from behind his desk Every teacher is a bent

gun barrel A voice thrower isn't a metaphor it's an ex
cuse to hang round the stage door begging for the pup
pet's autograph which he scratches into your arm with
hypodermic fairytale bondage thin as voice recognition prog.

Salved valve antique quake erupts in mute salvo Sand
man gang phenotype types reams of cute dream dictat
ion dictated by a democrat in dickeybow lake of balsa
mic thirst for hunger hung by its fums while minimalist ghost

writes his own ghost story about when capitalism pot
ted me in blood&bone in a market garden guarded by
wire barbs drawn in felt-tip Desire filled-in with conc
rete not mulch mocks-up a sleepy elegy with feet up slamming

already crumbling Tesco brand biscuits on desk next
door *Don't lay anything on my voice* is a quote when
in Cardiff do what the Roman Welsh do pretend tobe
watching boring match in the pub as if given a prescription by

Dr. Tension for Tennysonian lipgloss smeared across
a Turner Business proceeds curlingstone smooth curl
icue dizzy by linguistic linefeed back to stray demon
stration days of hendiadys and henpecked priests I was an Al

debaran owl onthebusback from Brum all eyes& ears
reading *Howl* bought in the Bull Ring while listening
to a loud teenage sister telling her little brother about
her sex experiments The world was howling and I was hungry.

Red-eyed Med tanned white by homenow holidaysun
turns its backtoback skyflack incandescing plastic im
agism choke navel fluff on Plymouth Navy Days pick
s at its pimples and winks at pimps in lilywhite changingroom

turned pink by Hitchcock missing a walk-on scene in
which he'd planned to lick an ice-cream off the straw
berry blond because he was called back to the battery
to recharge or face the colour dialled tide of off-white horses.

Yet edges of vision nudge your elboweye with e-bow
between two horizons You choose with your 3rd eye a
phenomenological blindspot seen heading home from
the scaffold with singularly handsome grin A sword without

a blade isn't harfassharp as a knife withoutanandle but
neither is Mr Everyman a sage in a topper strolling up
an avenue sucking a sweet sour behind his moustache
Schwitters takes assembly at art college but it's the wrong end

of the day so students in ebonyevil nemosilkkimonos
licktheirboottongues and stick them lizardly out grud
gingly to catch the coach an old banger-bus driven by
sandy haired Dr. Lopez decked out as Dick Whittington's cat

driving them without qualified witnesses to the moor
to chase the sun into a bebrambled brackpool of stem
drown gingered sacrifice like the sun was a minefield
of gilded fox ore Polite coughing from cherrywood coffin asks

for a caesarean The day's gone on toolong the witless
knight kicks spurs into eohippus andthe waiting night
purrs Nakedness gnaws into my shoulder bone Horse
chomps a raw russet Axed orchard bane Lucifer guests on *I L*

ove Lucy Memory full Mammary empty either way a
sleeping dog licks its blinking wounds linking back a
clean heel to bigbaddeath brandishing brushed leather
licence to kill issued by the Light Brigade's lawyer he charges

less for the team's awaystrip Caged pitpony sings Bar
ry's *Hellhound Memos* ittakesmeback to touch typing
at Connaught House Business Studies pitmanning my
own version of *Positively 4ᵗʰ St.* nervously manning an office

and splitting Anarchism's atomic billiard bustups into
free periods not quite the puremetaphysicalexperience
at the bus-stop or Joycean epiphany when Ms Hawley
sent me to get some milk with Audrey the mid-morning sun en

folded and fostered my orphaned soul &I never felt so
good for nothing on Earth We were freshly forged old
gold in an otherwise empty exercise book Pat Ella An
nette &theothers on empty lines too a business trip busman's

holiday in the cramped chatty library doing their nails
magenta as I recruited a Red Rudi army least 4 dawns
too early on beach battleground where 2 redflags pace
d themselves tween rival tides of local radio yawning into port

with red sky in mourning shepherd's warning logo on
a shivering mod under the pier Pete T had it to a T we
just wore PJ Proby t-shirts and the girls as always had
legs to run in no it never hurt my pirate blue stripes sandals &

skyblue cord hipsters + Uncle John's green waistcoat
What's important about the past that isn'tso at the tim
e imported from foolproof futures where a production
value has no need of a script Everything shrinks i.e. past gets

closer&closer until seas crease-up with zoomed muse
Pat's brother Paul was fiery referee Paul Durkin strut
ting along the road with his boots strangling him boun
cing the ball from foot t hand t foot t road t hand t road t hand

t foot to his brother then Pat pushed a pram past and I
peeped in Once too she picked me off the road where
I fell for her she grazed my eyes every day she kicked
with her orange hair and ran from the teacher on a last day of

term and made him cry she was still laughing tears on
the bus flushed with the thrill Their dad Dirty Durkin
played for Portland F.C. he still had an accent getting
slower&slower&dirtier&dirtier defending our stony box his

face redder&redder over the years but their mum lost
her head's red I mixherup with a Ginger Kelly whose
son another Paul had art talent but died young his you
nger sister had dark red curls framing the cheekiest face on the

island suddenly the same age as us as the happiest the
sun's ever seen rose grinning from a forest of freckles
We had Boot&Rusty frothy love we had everything in
an ungrouped gang for at least the dogs' hour breathing friendly

fire on any newly discovered planet Greengreen grow
the stones under the sea and close to me there is blood
in our hair no not there yes there that'sit that'sthe spot
that has disappeared under an avalanche of limestone cowboys.

So is this shake of the sauce bottle of memory upside
down the only source of a set sun or what sipped tom
ato soup from a stetson chance have we of looking ba
ck without going subconsciously blind? Torrid lobsterbed pel

vic conscience torrent Meerkat air guitars a cherryred
magiccarpet digitally ferreting away a rocksunder etc.
Prophesy skips lunch Recordbreaking runnerhasbeans
the VampPyresfromVenus wallowed in a can't play but am do

ing so anyway novelty swallowing garagefuls of holl
ow garbage 'cluding corn-on-the-cob butter burnt dirt
black they reform as Smutty Cupids but old hell itself
caught fire it had to be evacuated by a cast of rejuvenated Trist

an Tzaras I embarrassed Eleanor getting off her gram
mar bus by calling her by her red hair she waz my 11
yr.old ex it was my way of saying I love you as in the
Armitage poem about a hot ring I shocked myself it wasn't me

shouting rude fun it was *my science fiction twin* the 1
what passed the 11+ wearing their black and red slug
cap while my cap&blazer were serge grey only a bad
ge sported a black motto beside a red tie nobody from The Holy

Child cd read none of us was holy I hadn't quite read
Kerouac atthatpoint only a mewling geography book
I hadn't even read myself it took another 35 odd odd
years to download the game into my contagious brain A fringe

bogey process of random up a creek impiety is purely
as modest asisposs Ego snuggles like a tick into a can
can combustion where quantum space fills the engine
with a peace-keeper's tommyturds Sober despair spat forth 4x4

art crit copy but every 4th was an oath in the mouth of
a rhetorical oaf who never did get to sew his oats into
a Shreddy Old Labour old labour how lovely are your
branches? That oldtime politics over a pint of newtime religion.

World Warp 1 raps Beatles or Stones & Wapping lies
Robin Hood the redbreast freerunning along business
park roofs When the screws turned the otherway they
screwed the one with the screw loose Red Rum spook poked

cowpatter from an open-top halfdoor portrait halfway
up a grand staircase in a mansion full of aint-halfmad
prisoners running off so fast on the spot they've been
redshifted Tense not accruable when the languaged mind scan

ning timeless untruths hurls a decoy decree for a phil
ologist to digest its workmanlike nift e.g. a doggedly
calculated degree concludes: compared with a whore
a horse has a voice but hey hoe it's the hoarse throated heehaw

whore with a hobby but not a hubby painting a sunset
behind papiermâché hills The nag won't reach Vortic
ist trainingcamp by sunset or even by moonlight filter
ed blog waffle banging on about rights another narrative threat

ening to narrow a life like the poems bout mum&dad
that freeze a flatfish placebo into a sickbay mantaray
debating at the Oxford Union with snoozing chip pan
inorunder a cart on whether the alchemist's apprentice's voice

will ever breakornot New Labour broke-in recruits by
makinemlisten to a Spandau Ballet cruet débridement
set New Labourlout health minister how creepy are yr
hunches? I'd rather vote for the creatures living in the crap in

the garden come to think of it I'd rather vote for an an
imal's abandoned veto I can hear it in an updated void
of the hear&now winevoice grain indirt soulduff enuf
energy housed in chemical nostalgia for a hand-me-down love.

The animal's abandoned veto is a favourite track The
artwork's end Voltaire caught on *Candid Camera* fad
ing into fad on a death-bed made by a layabout guard
ian angel The artwork ends not knowing about snuff masks n

stuff I just guessed that attempts to throw voices willy
nilly will catcHiNthEthroaT's Schrödinger number on
a lottery rollover every hurtle to attention drilling ping
through trivia to time refracted in the balls' highlights as Draw

master John displays a hangman's patience&decorum
That's normal that is like a paranormal echo-rush past
ship's thrush rash to assemble after fire-drill on a new
born star skimming a rusty old sea Too much coy copying in

this universe My aesthetically atheist soul an up&pun
ning machine bought in PC World & Comet&Curry's
anywhere that swops detaled Devil smallprint for you
r details miniaturised for the poor to pour their hearts' savings

into as 'merica stinkbombs restoftheworld with moral
capital then craps our collective conscience on studio
floor Local sewer pipe slopes thataway past the point
of shared horizon to crudecrown crassgrab crudgate richwitch

rationed rationalism in which any individual hominid
has no relations except Adam and no one to play with
except Adam Smith The tide doesn't crawl it limpsup
the beach of this half-baked biography acting all trident strident

with fuckedfeet and forkedhands as the lifeguard blis
ters Lifebuoy pink and catcleaning clouds lickhot off
soapy foam around a hogwash sun The matt grey rain
warms *the cockles of your heart* and you really don't care who

you are it's the world out there that counts 2ten while
Britannia sits on her shield *ouch* then rolls a penny in
a slot machine that's already hooked a carefree beach
comber He dries his feet on a Union Jack colour cartridge he

needs changing after every printing of a motive motif
Everything makes sense that is a trouble starved child
can be explained victims far too understood for every
violence has its own magnetic vector Wisdom volunteers to be

helpless Celebrity illusionist hides but leaves his sex-
life on display she bends absorbing fragments of free
fall vision then spews a litter of throwaway ickytease
He sips red milk through a straw-pole The audience claps them

in jail Alien lands in chains on observatory floor He's
put to work forging DearJohns signed Billy No Mates
yet evenout in diurnal reality no starry-eyed shine pen
etrates paper If I was dead wrong I'd rather be dead&gone for

a long long time I'd set out my featherweight football
stall but stall selling them until a mighty matchball M
itre kicked from the car-park corner scattered them in
to azure Each ball an exile every kick an enigma helping out

with anything too technical suchasa son Life's far too
weird once the exotic bore is strained out leaving you
romantically abstract sponsorship gossiped by censor
ship of a Sociology-in-the-lab lecture on the barricades 1871.

Said at start it wouldn't bebout culture but corruption
caught beyond boundary isn't even a technicality The
cast of outcasts quit quidditch to play the usual poetry
stuff you know the trajectory you just havetohave the concept

ual coordination to pickitup&throwitback but the next
field's blasé about what the farmer does until it blazes
rasping ghosts but driving backdown the M5 the blaze
in the left field was *the quality of the light* this evening's ghost

of epiphany more pithy than youth's past so why take
comfort in begetting contradiction? A lost poem won
't be found in life or life prosed-up&stripped-down to
its dwarf locality On her first day on dry land a mermaid with

red weed hair keeps within port's environs to practise
walking up and down the street The radical old moon
coral brittle&bloodshot needs a service A little honey
drips from thepubthe Wound in the Wall known queer quietly

as thepubthe FornowAlllame University but mermaid
makes a mess of the entrance exam she writes it in cu
neiform inkling *I'm notevengoingtomakeit onto Prof.*
Slouch's professional motherhood class or sneak shallowswims

in inearly soggyroom then she lights up in an old film
asif that made her native in her own sunburnt story hu
mming asif human the song *the sea is distant memory*
Her own smell reminds her of forgetfulness Laundry fug&fog.

Her son is old nun but she fills him in with new know
ledge *your father was sweeperdreft navysurplus bride*
flightlessly dissatisfied and brewedtwice before break
Rotting rosette sun blames anyone for anything it's ever done.

The queue of those who don't belong here goes round
&round the world and they all have stuff too heldtight
as kids their patience exhausting to those watching W
imbledon from the top of Nepal or is it from the roof of a bar

gain 1up1down Barratt built on the site of demolished
labour camp Never imagined world would be like this
maybe a computerbit of civil war plus a *struggle to be*
human followed by a Durutti Column parade past my youngest

daughter's drawing of a beheaded headofstate buttwas
more than a wrong simulacrum getting spoofed a Rim
baud boots sale is always on down the stumps Hannah
Lawton destroyed by cancer&catholicism Iknowwhich got her

first Cemetery mudbathpath creosoted by gypsies bla
thering on hindleg horses ran free never ridden never
fed they eat the fields they drink the rain as simple as
that it doesn't matter what the blinkered DJ's amass in their fat

heads it all gets sold-on behind some carboot longwit
signed certs from MrMoorcock reject riddles framing
wall in its own skinned future A customer cameupout
of soccer sods asking *Anyreptilesoulsforsale?* Yes one I replied

but a bit shabby and in need of a scrub we rummaged
to the bottom of the box and lifted out a Lyme Bay at
sunset painted west from Portland the frame cheaper
than chicken-in-the-drain an amateur chip style crap colour gar

ish firstshave razor on a sea of pale grease slashed cal
low with a lazar but no sun there the ochre orange red
filled the horizon but cloudpurple occluded our sunny
star *I'll have it How much?* said the stranger *It's priceless you*

can have it and I meant it as he cut into my silhouette
with a rose Confidential terror broadcasts goosescore
flesh Comfy monochrome atrocity defence burnsbills
The submissive bastards succeed in their submission The voice

throws itself into heavily annotated failure it involves
a muchloved exspearmint volunteering anonymous pr
ofiling in brownpaperbag multiple rightangle stickout
It cutsout of mother searching for mum to find spasmodic buzz

exiled from selfabstraction &anyother anecdote or act
ion flailing Horuschorus the sea's not porous butitcan
zip up your future into a babygrow Suntart mammal's
innumerable encores polyphonic freegazeddiamondgeezer333.

★

Author's Notes

The Voice Thrower is from a batch of long poems begun in the '90s, arising in my "anti-poetry" phase. The title should speak for itself, except it doesn't, which is the whole point of being a voice thrower. The poem had a twin, *The Submissive Bastards*, initially sharing the trope of a red sky at dusk, but TVT's sky turned into a horizon at sea, specifically from Portland looking west across Lyme Bay (Portlanders call it West Bay anyway).

While *The Voice Thrower*'s bastard twin became more controlled, TVT grew ever wilder until, while trying to round it off, I began to suspect the poem was an unconscious attempt to engage with the memory of my mother (*Hannah Lawton*), yet I resisted making this the focus and let the poem mutate again, the original trope of the red horizon (my mother had red hair) spreading rhizome-like through the various scenarios. The irony though was that the more it tried to resist biography the more autobiographical it became.

*

Any attempt to supply comprehensive notes would be courting with the impossible (its "cast" comes to nearly 200) but the following references and acknowledgments might be helpful:

East Weirs and West Weirs — Areas on the Isle of Portland that lie between the cliffs of the main plateau of the island and the sea. The East Weirs are extensive but in my childhood were mostly restricted M.O.D. property. The West Weirs are smaller and narrower and mostly covered in huge rocks that have fallen from the quarried cliffs above. *The Green Hump*, which features twice in the poem, is a strange long mound lying at the far end of the West Weirs.

The Restaurant Joke — A long, unpublished prose poem written in my teens.

The square — Portland Square, which used to be regularly flooded after bad storms. *Mayo's café* was in the square and *Jimmy Mayo*, a son of the owners, was in my class. Recently I discovered he had been the manager of the hotel in Blandford at the same time as it hosted the Blandford Poetry Festivals (*Blandford fest*), an annual event which, for various reasons, still looms large in the memories of us Plymouth 'lager louts'.

David — David Cox, a close friend of childhood and teens, pops up a few times here. The lines "*duck alone on new moon with a beak bright brown / Plastic hoof throbbed like a swollen young balloon*" refer to two of our favourite images from his drawings. Went to London to see *Joan* (Joan Baez). *Boot&Rusty* were our dogs.

Millie Small — Jamaican singer who had hits in the '60s. At a Rolling Stones concert in Weymouth, 1964, she was the support act and she coaxed me onto the stage where I had to be her *Boy Lollypop*—I stood there like a pillock.

Tillycoombe — Tillycoombe Road, Portland where I lived from ages 2–12 before we moved to a council flat on another estate. After watching *Gone with the Wind* I used to lie awake imagining cannons firing down on our house from the heights of the *Verne's top tier* (Verne Prison) above. The scene in the film where *Scarlett O'Hara (Vivienne Leigh)* confronts *the grizzly Yankee sergeant* on the stairs haunted me for years (no idea why) then re-emerged with force while writing TVT.

cousin Kevin — I really do have a cousin Kevin but he's nothing like the lad in the Undertones' song; if anything our roles would have been reversed.

Dad and *burning banister* — A fire broke out in the middle of the night in a house near us and my dad was first on the scene. That same day I had been on a school trip from *Holy Child Secondary Mod* to *Longleat*.

The Devonport — The Devonport End at Plymouth Argyle, behind the goal.

'*in manner of catatonic tetra meter of ionics*' — From *The Chambers Dictionary*.

down along the Cove — Dylan song. *The Cove* also refers to the pub on the Chesil seawall where David and myself used to have *Half a Guinness&chips*. There is also a reference later to Dylan's *Positively 4th Street* in connection with my time at *Connaught House Business Studies* where I was a student with *Pat Ella An / nette &theothers*. On occasion we had to sit in the office, answer the phone and do officey things but when it was my turn I spent it writing my own verses to *Positively 4th Street*, because I didn't think the original was long enough. In our free periods in the *chatty library*, when we were supposed to be studying, the girls would be *doing their nails / magenta* while I read books about anarchism and atomic particles: *Anarchism's atomic billiard bustups*.

Hardy's Monument — the monument in commemoration of Admiral Hardy built high on the downs in Dorset. On clear days it could be seen from our window, ten miles away. For me it represented the point at which the rest of the world began.

Marlborough Primary — School in a very deprived area of Devonport where I taught from 1988 to 1993, when I had a breakdown.

Lenkiewicz — Robert Lenkiewicz, the painter. He deigned to let us use his studio once for a reading by Maggie O'Sullivan and Tom Raworth. A strange man, to say the least. I was jealous of his rare book collection (dusty tomes of dark philosophy), which is why I imagine him having a priceless edition of *The Famous Five*.

Melmoth — 'Melmoth the Wanderer', gothic novel by Charles Maturin.

Melcombe Regis — An area of *Weymouth*, though when I wrote this I was actually thinking of Wyke Regis, another area of Weymouth, the one I travelled through most days of my early life, it's just that *Melcombe* sounded better with *Melmoth*. I always associated a scene from Melmoth the Wanderer with the lyrics to *Captain Beefheart's (Van Vliet's) Bat Chain Puller*, from the album *Shiny Beast*, and pictured the mad procession going down Wyke Road. I also name check Beefheart's *Run Paint Run Run*, from 'Doc at the Radar Station'.

Trend — This refers to a local mod group who used to play in venues around Weymouth in the mid '60s. They called themselves Trend 66 in '66 and Trend 67 in '67 etc. A series of convoluted associations, e.g. the *generic ginger beardbiscuit*, surround them in the poem.

Don't lay anything on my voice — A quote from Alice Notley. When I returned to TVT in an attempt to pull it together I was also immersed in Alice's 'Alma or The Dead Woman' (Granary

2006), another long, mad poem. (My review of it can be found on the Intercapillary Space blog archive.) The result was that it overly influenced the ending of TVT, necessitating a rewrite of the final pages. Nevertheless, the sudden intrusion of a narrative concerning the *mermaid with //red weed hair* owes something to Alice Notley's metamorphic female characters, though this particular mermaid is also Sticking Plaster, a mermaid that comes up for air in some of my other poems.

Pat's brother Paul was fiery referee Paul Durkin — Football fans would know that Paul Durkin became a top-flight F.A. referee. It was writing the lines about remembering him as a kid *strut / ting along the road with his boots strangling him boun / cing the ball from foot t hand* that in the original draft first broke away from associative sound abstractions towards the more concrete.

Armitage poem — 'I am very bothered when I think' by Simon Armitage.

science fiction twin — 'My Science Fiction Twin' by Elvis Costello, from the album 'Brutal Youth'.

Spandau Ballet cruet — This was a real dream (as opposed to an unreal one) in which the members of Spandau Ballet were represented by a five piece cruet set. I can still see their round little Spandau faces depicted on the cruets—three salts and two peppers obviously.

*

Finally, if *The Voice Thrower* is as difficult to read as it was to write, you have my sympathy, although any correspondence with regard to form, new word compounds or spelling should be turned into a paper boat and pushed off Chesil Beach at sunset.

Tim Allen
1 December 2011

www.ingramcontent.com/pod-product-compliance
Lightning Source LLC
Chambersburg PA
CBHW031929080426
42734CB00007B/615